Ismail Gadzhiev
Elnur Kalbizadeh

From the history of diplomacy

Ismail Gadzhiev
Elnur Kalbizadeh

From the history of diplomacy

Nakhchivan diplomats

ScienciaScripts

Imprint

Cover image: www.ingimage.com

This book is a translation from the original published under ISBN 978-3-330-33178-5.

Publisher:
Sciencia Scripts
is a trademark of
Dodo Books Indian Ocean Ltd. and OmniScriptum S.R.L publishing group

120 High Road, East Finchley, London, N2 9ED, United Kingdom
Str. Armeneasca 28/1, office 1, Chisinau MD-2012, Republic of Moldova, Europe
Managing Directors: Ieva Konstantinova, Victoria Ursu
info@omniscriptum.com

Printed at: see last page
ISBN: 978-620-8-40492-5

PROMINENT NAKHCHIVANS

- WHOSE DIPLOMATIC WORK IS A SOURCE OF PRIDE

Diplomacy is not a profession. It is a field of art that requires, like art, composer's art, carpet weaving, calligraphy, a special innate talent. Here a mistake in one sketch, in one notation, in one loop, in one ornament can ruin the whole work. That is why they say that one cannot become a diplomat, one must be born a diplomat.

One of the most important issues facing modern Azerbaijani historio-graphy is the study of the history of diplomacy, analysis of the lives and activities of diplomats who played an important role in the history of Azerbaijan. The Nakhchivan region, which has historically given outstanding personalities to Azerbaijan, is also the birthplace of a number of outstanding diplomats.

Nakhchivan province is located in a geostrategic territory, which has always been within the circle of interests of neighboring states and major powers. This region, which was once geographically one of the central territories of Azerbaijan, by the verdict of history, due to the interest of major powers in different epochs, was either a part of these powers or was independent.

The 19th and 20th centuries were the most difficult and complex for the Nakhchivan region. When the Russian Empire occupied the South Caucasus, including Azerbaijan, one of the most important places here was Nakhchivan. Although Nakhchivan was not occupied by the Treaty of Gulustan, concluded after the first war between Russia and Qajar Iran between these two states, the Turkmen-Chay Treaty, concluded as a result of the subsequent war between these two states, also included the territory of Nakhchivan into the Russian Empire. Nakhchivan was not only occupied, but its demography also changed.

After the occupation from Qajar Iran and the Ottoman Empire, along with Yerevan, Karabakh, thousands of Armenian families were resettled to the territory of Nakhchivan.

The tragedies of the Nakhchivans and the loss of their lands took place later on.

The Armenian Dashnaks, who relied on the patronage of the great powers and received moral and material support from them, made attempts to realize their intentions to seize Nakhchivan. The Armenian Dashnaks, who had created their own state in the territory of Azerbaijan with the assistance of imperialist forces, also liked Nakhchivan. The Armenians, who planted the idea that "without Nakhchivan and Sharur Armenia cannot survive", resorted to the military way at the beginning of the XX century.

Political and state figures of Azerbaijan, as well as Nakhchivan, opposed the illusions of Armenian Dashnaks in their activities. None of the Nakhchivan political and state figures we have mentioned had diplomatic education. But the situation in which they found themselves and the unjust claims to Nakhchivan made them diplomats. Some of them did not even have sufficient experience in this field. Nevertheless, as part of their activities, they fought resolutely for the territorial integrity of Azerbaijan as well as Nakhchivan.

When it comes to Nakhchivan diplomats, the first person who comes to mind is Behbud agha Shahtakhtinsky. He also had no diplomatic or any other serious education. But his diplomatic activity in the direction of gaining autonomy for Nakhchivan, preserving Nakhchivan as an integral part of Azerbaijan can cast a shadow on the work of dozens of diplomats. Thanks to this countryman, who largely determined the fate of Nakhchivan, this region did not fall under Armenian occupation.

Ibrahim Abilov, Magomed Khan Tekinski, Bahram Khan Nakhchivanski acted in defense of Azerbaijan's national interests as professional diplomats. They were also closely connected with diplomatic activity. Some less, some more, all of them were engaged in this field and always attracted attention with their activities.

Although some prominent Nakhchivans, being representatives of various professions, were not actively engaged in diplomatic activities, they also devoted this activity to our national interests, the struggle for the territorial integrity of our state.

The toughness of Ali Sabri Gasimov's answers to the British and American representatives, the decisiveness of his position, the seriousness of his actions are indispensable qualities of a true diplomat. We can say the same about others.

In general, we are indebted to the diplomatic activity of the mentioned political and state figures - Nakhchivans for the fact that in the early 20th century the

Nakhchivan region did not fall into the hands of an insidious enemy and remained Azerbaijani territory. Therefore, we should always remember them, study their activities and inform the young generation about them.

From the authors

Nakhchivan diplomats

MUHAMMED AGHA SHAHTAKHTINSKY

It is said that there are three Shakhtakhts in Nakhchivan. The first one is the top of Elinje Mountain, where the throne of the Eldegisids was once kept. The second is the place in the village of Jehri, where Nadir Shah once addressed his soldiers. The third is the village on the Sharur plain, now part of the Kengerli district of the Nakhchivan Autonomous Republic. Here Shah Ismail Khatai won the last key victory that brought him to the Shah's throne. In other words, after

Shakhtakhty was the place where military leaders, diplomats and healers who were in Ismail's headquarters gathered for the Battle of Sharur. Who knows, perhaps that is why this small village later gave the world prominent diplomats, military leaders, physicians, writers....

Speaking about diplomats of Shakhtakhty village, it is customary to mention first of all a prominent political figure of the early XX century Behbud

Shahtakhtinsky. But we have data that writer Muhammad Shahtakhtinsky, who was one of the first to present the problem of Azerbaijani identity to the public, worked for some time in the diplomatic service as an interpreter.

M. Shakhtakhtinsky was born in 1846, graduated from the Tiflis Classical Gymnasium and then studied at the Faculty of History, Philosophy and Law of the University of Leipzig, the center of higher experiential education of the famous Sorbonne. He spoke Russian, German, French, Arabic, Persian and Greek, and also knew a number of dead languages - Pahlavi, Zendi and Latin.

So far, the literature has mainly covered the period of M. Shakhtakhtinsky's life in 1909-1912 as a time of diplomatic work. But it should be pointed out that even before that - in the late 1880s Muhammed agha Shahtakhtinsky worked as a permanent representative of the Russian Empire in the International Commercial Court, the headquarters of which was located in Istanbul. This position allowed him to become deeply acquainted with the social and political life of the Ottoman state. M.Shahtakhtinsky translated into Russian and published a treatise by the former Ottoman ambassador to Russia Adjutant General Ahmed Shakir "Calculation of solar chronology in the Muslim world". In the article of academician I.Habibbeyli "Muhammed agha Shahtakhtinsky: roads of fate and merits" it is noted that, according to some data, Muhammed Shahtakhtinsky also translated the book of Ahmed Dzhevdet on the history of Muslim religion.

In 1907, M. Shahtakhtinsky was elected as a deputy to the Russian State Duma from Iravan province. Courageously defending the interests of the inhabitants of his native land in the distant northern capital, he simultaneously had the opportunity to closely observe the social and political life of Russia.

In 1909-1912, Muhammed agha Shahtakhtinsky worked as a journalist-translator at the Russian Embassy in Istanbul. Using his diplomatic status, he established contacts with some high-ranking officials of the Ottoman Empire, learned their point of view on topical issues and prepared newspaper materials on this basis. Thus, in 1908, the newspaper "Russkoye Slovo" published an interview with the Minister of Religious Affairs of the Ottoman Empire Shemseddin bey. In addition, M. Shahtakhtinsky was engaged in translations of documents and works on military and political topics. His most serious work in this direction is considered to be the translation into Russian of the book "History of the Russian-Turkish War of 1877-1878 in Asia Minor" by the commander-in-chief of the Ottoman army Mukhtar Pasha. As Azerbaijani historian Musa Guliyev points out, translated excerpts of this book were published in 1913-1916 in the Russian journal "Journal of Military History". However, the discontinuation of the journal did not allow the entire work to be published.

Upon his return to his homeland in 1915, M.Shahtakhtinsky also worked as an interpreter in the diplomatic service. According to Azerbaijani historian Shovgi Novruzov, he headed the Eastern Department of the Russian Foreign Ministry for some time. However, subsequent research showed that M.Shahtakhtinsky actually worked in the Foreign Ministry system as an interpreter of the 7th category until he retired in 1917.

Under the Azerbaijan Democratic Republic, Muhammad Agha worked mainly as a journalist and in the field of education, and after Sovietization he worked as an adviser on special issues to the Chairman of the Soviet of People's Commissars of the Azerbaijan SSR Nariman Narimanov. According to academician Isa Habibbeyli, M.Shahtakhtinsky was one of the main organizers of the Congress of the Peoples of the East held in Baku.

Muhammad aga Shakhtakhtinsky died on December 12, 1931. The location of his grave is unknown, which is also a subject of research for historians.

MOHAMMED KHAN OF TEKE

When he was born, no one could have imagined that soon a war would break out that would radically change his destiny, taking him far away from his homeland, where he would grow up and then devote his life to the good and safety of his new homeland. His biography will prove that homeland is not necessarily the place where you were born, it is much more important to become attached, attached to your soul and imbued with a sense of belonging.

Magomed Khan of Teke was born in 1879 or 1880 in the Trans-Caspian valley of Akhaltek, when the war between the Turkmen and Russia was going on there. However, it happened that the boy was adopted by Ehsan Khan of Nakhchivan, one of the most influential chiefs of the Azerbaijani tribe of Kengerli, and grew up in Nakhchivan. Until recently, the date of his birth remained unknown until Azerbaijani scientist Atakhan Pashayev discovered the personal file of Magomed Tekinsky, a student of the Law Faculty of Novorossiysk University, in the State Archive of Odessa region of Ukraine. It should be noted that some other prominent Azerbaijani public figures of the early 20th century, who played a significant role in the history of the Nakhchivan region - Aziz-bek Gadimbekov, secretary of the Consulate of the Azerbaijan Democratic Republic in Batumi, Aligulu-khan Kalbalikhanov, Idayat-bek Sultanov, Hamid-bek Shahtakhtinsky - studied at the same university.

In the article of A.Pashayev "Who is Magomed-khan Tekinski?" it is noted: "In the information about the students of the first gymnasium of Tiflis city against the surname of M.Tekinsky in the column of the father's name is indicated "Ehsan-khan Tekinsky", in the column of the guardian's name - "Jafargulu-khan of Nakhchivan", nationality - Turkmen, religion - Muslim, year of birth - 1879".

On January 12, 1881, during the siege of the Turkmen fortress Goitepe by Russian troops, all of Magomed's relatives were killed, and he was found in a haystack by the Russian army colonel Ehsan-khan and adopted. According to the materials of Azerbaijani historian, employee of Nakhchivan branch of ANAS Musa Guliyev, Ehsan-khan took the boy with him to Nakhchivan, and here he grew up under the supervision of Jafargulu-khan, Rahim-khan and Huseyn-khan of Nakhchivan. He graduated from the first men's gymnasium in Tiflis, and in 1908 graduated from the law faculty of the Novorossiysk Imperial University in Odessa. We know virtually nothing about Magomed Khan's studies during the next ten years. The same M.Guliyev, after working in the Russian State Military History Museum in Moscow and the Russian State History Archive in St. Petersburg, established that M.Tekinsky served in the Russian army after graduating from the gymnasium. A.Pashayev concluded on the basis of the materials of the State Archive of Odessa region that after graduating from Novorossiysk University he worked in the law enforcement agencies of Transcaucasia. The scientist proceeded from the fact that on July 15, 1918, Magomed Khan was involved in the Extraordinary Investigation Commission of the ADR government in Ganja as a sworn assessor. This commission was established to investigate the facts of violence against the Muslim population of the whole Transcaucasia and robberies of their property since the period of the First World War. Along with Magomed Khan Tekinsky, the commission included Alekper-bek Hasmamedov, Andrei Fomich Novatsky, Nikolai Mikhailovich Mikhailov, Alexander Kluge, Ismail-bek Shakhmaliev, Alei Adamovich Alexandrovich, Czeslaw Boleslavovich Klossovsky, V.V. Goodwill, Abbasali-beg Haji Irzaev.

The greatest merits of Mohammed Khan Tekin to Azerbaijan are given to the period of the Azerbaijan Democratic Republic. In the first government of the republic, he was temporarily entrusted with the duties of the Minister of Foreign Affairs. In addition, according to an archive document cited in the fifth volume of the seven-volume book "History of Azerbaijan", he was also a member of parliament: "Member of the Azerbaijani parliament, Magomed-khan Tekinski was appointed ambassador to Iravan on January 29, 1919. In this post he worked honorably until October of the same year. In the book "Azerbaijan Democratic Republic and Nakhchivan" we read: "Being unable to take military measures in connection with Nakhchivan, the ADR government resorted to some political and diplomatic measures. .... In connection with Nakhchivan M. Tekinski wrote to the Chairman of ADR government that if Armenia agrees to transfer Karabakh to Azerbaijan, the British will give it Sharur-Nakhchivan. In his opinion, it was impossible to do this, as the majority of the population of Sharur and Nakhchivan were Muslims. M. Tekinsky also had great merits in suppressing self-rule of Armenians in Nakhchivan province. He prepared reports on this issue and sent them to the Ministry of Foreign Affairs".

On October 1, 1919, M.Tekinski was appointed Deputy Minister of Foreign Affairs of Azerbaijan and remained in this position until the fall of ADR. While in this position, he took part in negotiations with the Polish representative in the Caucasus Vaclav Ostrovsky, the British High Commissioner to the Caucasus Oliver Wardrop, and the Extraordinary Mission of Poland.

The fate of Mohammed Khan of Teke after April 1920 is unknown. His name is found only in the list of those shot and arrested for 1937-1938, compiled by historian Adalat Tairzade. Against it is stamped: 18.03.1938, 58 years old. Above the date there is an asterisk, which, as the author's note informs us, means the date of execution.

BAKHRAM KHAN OF NAKHCHIVAN

Speaking at the conference on the occasion of the 90th anniversary of Azerbaijan's diplomatic service, Chairman of the Supreme Majlis of the Nakhchivan Autonomous Republic Vasif Talibov noted in particular: "Minister of Foreign Affairs of the Araz-Turkic Republic Bahram khan Nakhchivan, who made great efforts to reunite territorially isolated Nakhchivan with the Azerbaijan Democratic Republic, waged an active struggle to defend the territory of the state".

Bahram Khan of Nakhchivan occupies a worthy place among outstanding Azerbaijani diplomats. So far, researchers have focused on his merits as a military officer and in administrative management, but during the ADR period (1918-1920) Bahram-khan was engaged in diplomatic work for some time. During this period, in order to prevent pogroms of peaceful Azerbaijani population in Nakhchivan region by Dashnaks, Araz-Turkic Republic was formed and Bahram-khan as the head of delegation of this state conducted negotiations with both ADR delegation and Commander of Entente troops in Caucasus General V.Thomson, and in Tiflis with representatives of Georgian government. He took part in negotiations on the possibility of discussing the Nakhchivan issue at the Paris Peace Conference. Azerbaijani historian Musa Guliyev in his article "Aman-Khan of Nakhchivan: a personality we should know and familiarize with others" notes that Bahram Khan was born in 1872 in Nakhchivan, his father was Aman-Khan of Nakhchivan and his mother was

Fatmabike, granddaughter of Karabakh Mehtigulu Khan. By the way, Fatmabike khanum is the daughter of the famous Azerbaijani poetess Khurshidbanu Natavan.

Under tsarist rule, Bahram-khan worked in various positions: assistant police bailiff in the Nakhchivan district police department, honorary caretaker of the Nakhchivan Muslim school, member of the board of the world court in Nakhchivan. During the existence of the Araz-Turkic Republic he was not only one of the commanders of the people's militia, but also led the foreign policy of this republic. On January 25, 1919 Bahram-khan was appointed to the post of Minister of Foreign Affairs, and already in the first days of his new post he met with the members of the American commission that arrived from Iravan. In the course of negotiations an agreement was reached to open a 50-bed hospital in Nakhchivan, as well as to establish an orphanage for 250 children and allocate 50 thousand rubles and 4 thousand poods of wheat for its needs. Soon an orphanage for 200 places was opened in Nakhchivan.

The most important episode of Bahram Khan's diplomatic activity known to us today is his trip to Baku as the head of the delegation of the Araz-Turkic Republic in March 1919 to negotiate with the ADR government. Among the members of the delegation were such famous names as prominent Azerbaijani poet and playwright Huseyn Javid and writer, translator, one of the active participants of the national liberation movement Ali Sabri. As it is noted in the second volume of the encyclopedia "Azerbaijan Democratic Republic" published in 2005, on his way to Baku Bahram Khan Nakhchivan stopped in Tiflis, where he met with Georgian officials, and then in Ganja with representatives of the national movement, discussing the prospects of reunification of the Araz-Turkic Republic with the ADR. In Tiflis, according to Turkish author I. Atnur, he held talks with representatives of the British mission regarding the future borders of Nakhchivan province. He also met with Pasha Bayramov and Yusuf-bek Gaziyev, who had traveled to Baku as representatives of the Araz-Turkic Republic somewhat earlier, and introduced himself as the new Foreign Minister.

In the book of Azerbaijani historian Aydin Hajiyev "From the History of Kars and Araz-Turkic Republic" it is indicated that the delegation of the Araz-Turkic Republic headed by Bahram Khan of Nakhchivan held negotiations with the Prime Minister of ADR F.Khoysky, as a result of which the Azerbaijani government decided to send a group of 10 officers headed by Colonel Kugushev to the Araz-Turkic Republic. These officers took part in strengthening the defense of Nakhchivan province. In addition, Bahram Khan succeeded in sending a civilian delegation to Nakhchivan to familiarize with the difficult situation of the region and allocate one million rubles to cover the basic needs of the population. Thus, the government sent Teymur-bey Makinsky, R.Ismayilov and Dr. Ganizadeh to Nakhchivan, Sharur, Surmali, Vedibasar and Milistan districts, who were accompanied by representatives of the population of the region. The sources mention the names of Bagir Rzayev, Magerram Aliyev, Aliyashraf Kazimov, Huseyn Javid, Asad Manafov, as well as Bahram Khan and Aziz Khan of Nakhchivan.

Later Bahram-khan for some time held the post of assistant to the governor-general of Nakhchivan, and then the representative of the Ministry of Internal Affairs of Azerbaijan in Lankaran. With his organizational abilities he made a worthy contribution to the operation on defeat of White Guard detachments in Lankaran zone in August 1919 under the command of Major-General Habib bey Selimov. The Governor-General of Lankaran during this period was Javad-bek Melik-Yeganov.

After the Sovietization of Azerbaijan in April 1920, B.Nakhchivansky emigrated to Iran and lived in Tabriz. According to historian M.Guliyev, he was a member of anti-Soviet emigrant group and organization "Independent Caucasus". Unfortunately, we have no information about the time and place of death of Bahram Khan of Nakhchivan.

ALI SABRI GASSYMOV

"For three days and three nights I was in Tiflis writing a memorandum to General Gaskell....I handed the memorandum to the general."

Most often we remember him as a writer, journalist and translator, as a fighter for the freedom of Nakhchivan. In these days, when the 90th anniversary of Nakhchivan's self-determination is being widely celebrated, it is impossible not to recall the diplomatic activity of Ali Sabri Gasimov. Had it not been for him and other patriots who fought hard for their native land in 1918-1919, who reminded the American generals that they were military men, not rulers, the autonomy of the region in 1924 would have been under great doubt. If the people themselves do not fight for their future, no one from outside will come and grant them independence or other benefits. The autonomy of Nakhchivan is an important historical achievement, and the authors of it are the outstanding public and political figures of this region Kalbali-khan, Rahim-khan, Behbud Shahtakhtinsky, Ali Sabri Gasimov and others.

Ali Sabri Gasimov was born in 1892 in the village of Negram, which has long been famous for the militancy and unyielding character of its inhabitants. He studied at the Nakhchivan school of the famous Azerbaijani educator Magomed Tagi Sidgi, and then at the famous Gori Teachers' Seminary. His literary work is reported in detail in a number of articles and in the book "Ali Sabri" by Dr. Huseyn Hashimli, Doctor of Philological Sciences.

From the trenches to the negotiating table.....

The diplomatic activity of Ali Sabri Gasimov fell on 19181919 years - one of the most difficult periods in the history of Azerbaijan as a whole, when in the conditions of open claims of Armenian Dashnaks to the

A stubborn struggle for this ancient Azerbaijani region unfolded in Nakhchivan. All this prompted Ali Sabri Gasimov to rise to the defense of his native land. In previous sources, his diplomatic activity is described mainly on the example of meeting with the American General Gaskel, in fact, A.S.Gasimov also met with the Prime Minister of the Azerbaijan Democratic Republic Nasib Bey Yusufbeyli and Foreign Minister Mammad Yusif Jafarov. On September 9, 1919, he signed an appeal to the government of ADR on behalf of the population of Nakhchivan, Ordubad, Sharur, Surmali and Vedibasar districts.

The general recognized that he is a military man, not a politician.....

At the Tiflis meeting with American General Gaskel, Ali Sabri Gasimov made statements that characterize him not only as a fiery patriot, but also as a true diplomat, well versed in the interaction of politics and military sphere. Azerbaijani historian Musa Kuliyev in his article "Some notes about the hero of our history Ali Sabri Gasimov" reports that A.S.Gasimov handed a memorandum to Gaskel on behalf of Nakhchivan residents and said: "If these demands are not satisfied, Nakhchivans will defend their independence with arms in their hands". This memorandum was drawn up and handed over in response to the actions of the American military, which had arrived in the region, trying to take control of affairs in their own hands, and in case of failure were going to transfer the original Azerbaijani territories, including Nakhchivan, Ordubad, Sharur, Surmali and Vedibasar districts, to Armenia. Shortly before that, the British command in the region made an attempt to establish an Armenian administration in Nakhchivan, but it failed miserably, the local population strongly declared that the region was an integral part of Azerbaijan. General Gaskell, who arrived in the Caucasus and settled with his headquarters in Tiflis, held negotiations with the Azerbaijani government in Baku in early August on the creation of a buffer zone around Nakhchivan and the establishment of an American governorship there. As a result of the talks, a 12-point agreement was reached. According to Turkish author Ibrahim Ethem Atnur's book "Nakhchivan from Ottoman rule to Soviet rule (1918-1920)", the Azerbaijani government agreed to establish a temporary governorship-general. According to the agreement, the courts, railroads, highways, post and telegraph, and educational institutions in the territory of the governor-general's office were to be under the jurisdiction of the National Council in Nakhchivan, the budget was to be provided by the ADR treasury, Azerbaijani money was to be the official currency, and the construction site of the Baku-Julfa railroad was to be placed under Azerbaijani control.

However, on his return to Tiflis, Gaskell signed a completely different 21-point document contradicting the legitimate interests of Azerbaijan and at the same time opening space for Armenia's territorial claims, which was sent to the governments of Azerbaijan and Armenia. Having received the proposals of the Armenian side, the brave general accepted such conditions as transfer of the Daralaghez section to Armenia instead of including it in the neutral zone, recognition of Armenia as a privileged party in the future neutral zone, prohibition for Azerbaijan to send its money here, refusal to allow Azerbaijan the Baku-Julfa railroad, recognition of Zangezur district as an Armenian region. In parallel, Gaskell began to threaten the government of Azerbaijan, making it clear that he would not help against the danger from the north. In such an atmosphere A.S.Gasimov and a resident of Nakhchivan who was named Askerov as authorized representatives of Priaraksin Muslims went to Tiflis in the middle of September 1919 and met with General Gaskel. Before that, A.S.Gasymov met with the Prime Minister of Azerbaijan Nasib Bey Yusufbeylim, confirming the loyalty of the Nakhchivans to the ADR.

In previous publicistic and research works on this topic, two variants of the number of articles of the memorandum handed to Gaskel are given - 10 and 17. Academician Ismail Hajiyev's book "Azerbaijan Democratic Republic and Nakhchivan" and the already mentioned work by I.Atnur speak about 10 articles. This version, based on the materials of the Central State Archive of Modern History of Azerbaijan, seems to be closer to the truth.

The memorandum stipulated, in particular, the issues of holding a referendum in the Muslim priaraksin areas and the consent of the population to the establishment of the American governor-general's office only until the Paris Peace Conference confirmed the belonging of the region to Azerbaijan. Thanks primarily to the persistence of A.S.Gasimov and in the face of irrefutable arguments presented by him,

Gaskel made an unusual confession. Here is how the meeting with General Gaskel is described in Ali Sabri Gasimov's work "Memories, Experiences" published in the November 1982 issue of the magazine "Azerbaijan" - the organ of the Union of Writers of Azerbaijan: "In 1919, when the Entente troops occupied Transcaucasia, the commander was American General Gaskel. At that time the power in Armenia passed into the hands of the Dashnak party. The situation in Nakhchivan was tense, people could travel to Baku and Tiflis only through Zangezur. The Nakhchivans sent an elderly man named Askerov to me by this way. Three days and three nights I was in Tiflis writing a memorandum to General Gaskel. ...I handed the memorandum to the General. The interpreters gave the general the content of what was written.
He was brooding. I was looking out the window. The general was thinking about something with his head down. Finally, he looked up:

- Tell Mr. Sabri I'm a soldier. I don't do politics.

Two days later, local newspapers printed details of the negotiations under the headlines "Nakhchivan delegates at Gaskel's". Askerov bought several copies of the newspaper and returned to Nakhchivan".

The Azerbaijani government will not participate in a plan that the people of Nakhchivan do not want

Later, thanks to the negotiations with American representatives in Nakhchivan and the stubborn resistance of the people of the region, the U.S. was unable to achieve its goals in the region. This resistance gave the ADR government an important bargaining chip to reject the plan imposed on it. On the eve of the establishment of the stipulated U.S. governorship-general, the Azerbaijani side stated: "The government of Azerbaijan will not participate in a plan that the people of Nakhchivan do not want."

In the article "Ali Sabri Gasimov - half-forgotten diplomat, warrior, writer" by Azerbaijani historian Nail Aliyev, the following quote of A.S.Gasimov's dialog with High Commissioner in Transcaucasia Gaskel, taken from the 193rd issue of the government newspaper "Azerbaijan" for 1919, is given: "Nakhchivan will defend its independence with arms in its hands until the last breath. We do not recognize the state named Armenia. We reject such a state with all our strength because we want self-determination..... This is our right and we will not concede it to anyone. The people who have achieved freedom will not allow even the government of Azerbaijan to decide their fate without taking into account their will. This must be taken into account".

As a logical continuation of Ali Sabri Gasimov's demand for self-determination, which expressed the will of the population of Nakhchivan, the demand for autonomy of another prominent political figure from Nakhchivan, Behbud Shahtakhtinsky, arose some time later. It was due to the autonomy that the historical Azerbaijani face of ancient Nakhchivan was preserved. As a result, this region gave the world the greatest Azerbaijani of all times - Heydar Aliyev. This remarkable political and state figure knew well the history of Nakhchivan, including the factors accompanying the region's independence. And this knowledge saved Nakhchivan from Armenian occupation in the 90s of the last century.

BECHBUD SHAKHTAKHTINSKY

Behbud Shahtakhtinsky is a figure whose information about his life and political activities was scarce and contradictory until recently. Only the order of the Chairman of the Supreme Majlis of the Nakhchivan Autonomous Republic Vasif Talibov dated February 21, 2011 helped to establish and concretize his true place in the history of Azerbaijan.

When familiarizing myself with the literature on B. Shakhtakhtinsky, several circumstances caught my attention. Perhaps the most notable is that Behbud Shahtakhtinsky, born in 1881 in Shahtakhty village of Sharur district in a generic family, enjoyed high authority and respect among the so-called common people - peasants and workers. According to Azerbaijani historian, Doctor of Philosophy in History Musa Guliyev, in 1859 the commission on the cameral census of the Russian government in its resolution indicated: "According to the 1859 census, they are listed as beks. The members of the commission unanimously confirmed that even their great-grandfathers were from the nobility. They noted that the Shakhtakhtinskys belonged to the Gazakhlar tribe and that their great-grandfathers were descendants of Agajir-aga. So far, no one from this family has been deprived of bekstvo". Apparently, the innate deep sense of patriotism and love for his people, without distinction on social grounds, helped B.Shakhtakhtinsky to retain his authority even under the political regime that aimed to eliminate the "exploiting classes".

Leadership qualities and deep intelligence inherent in all representatives of the

Shahtakhtinski-Kengerli family allowed Behbud-aga to take part in the creation of the organization of office workers at the age of 24, and at the age of 36 to become a member of the executive committee of the Baku Council and the emergency commission of the "Baku Council of People's Commissars", chairman of the central council of the "Hummet" party.

After the Sovietization of Azerbaijan in 1920, Behbud-aga Shahtakhtinsky acted as the People's Commissar of Justice and at the same time was the extraordinary representative of the ASSR to the RSFSR. He did not have not only diplomatic but even ordinary secondary education, and yet, thanks to his innate talent and life experience, he achieved more than many educated people.

When studying the biography of B. Shakhtakhtinsky, it turns out that three factors played a major role in his formation as a diplomat - innate abilities, environment and necessity, i.e. life itself. It has long been known that life often teaches a person what books and pedagogues cannot teach. The qualities necessary for a successful diplomat - foresight, analytical gift and persistence in achieving the goal - were inherited from his glorious ancestors. His environment taught him to delve deeply into political events and use them for the benefit of his people. In fact, his ability to turn problems into opportunities is evident from his extensive report to Lenin on Azerbaijan, the situation in the Caucasus, Iran and Turkey, written in July-September 1920. This ability of B.Shahtakhtinsky can be seen in the signing of the agreement on military and economic union between the Azerbaijan SSR and the RSFSR, as well as the Moscow and Kars negotiations in 1921.

As for the factor of necessity, thanks to which B.Shahtakhtinsky became a prominent Azerbaijani diplomat, it is necessary to point to the crucial importance for Azerbaijan of the Nakhchivan issue in the negotiations between the RSFSR and the Republic of Turkey. On the other hand, the very fact of wide outlook and extensive knowledge, as well as patriotism in spite of sincere Bolshevik beliefs also served as an imperative for B.Shahtakhtinsky to become one of the prominent Azerbaijani diplomats.

When signing the Moscow Treaty between the RSFSR and Turkey on March 16, 1921, the protection of interests of Azerbaijan and Nakhchivan region at the highest level is undoubtedly the merit of Behbud Shahtakhtinsky in the first place. It is indicative that the second and third articles devoted to the issues of Batumi and Nakhchivan became the most important provisions of this document. It was due to the hard efforts of B.Shahtakhtinsky that the status and approximate borders of Nakhchivan province were stipulated in the third article of the agreement and annex 1 (c). In a letter from N.Narimanov we read: "Thank you for Nakhchivan! You see, you have already entered this work and are doing it correctly. This pleases me". The People's Commissar of Foreign Affairs of the Azerbaijan SSR Mirza Davud Huseynov also telegraphed to B.Shakhtakhtinsky, noting the importance of the Moscow Treaty.

Shahtakhtinsky's farsightedness as a diplomat was also clearly demonstrated during the signing of the Treaty of Kars. Many researchers criticize the position of B.Shahtakhtinsky, who at the negotiations in Kars opposed the signing of separate treaties between Turkey and the Caucasian republics. The Turkish side insisted on this during the 18-day negotiations, but the RSFSR, acting as a mediator, opposed it. Thus, B.Shahtakhtinsky actually supported the Russian position. However, had it not been for this position of the Azerbaijani diplomat, the Treaty of Kars would most likely not have gone beyond the boundaries of a mere bilateral document and would not have acquired the regional significance it has. Thanks to the purposeful diplomatic work of B.Shahtakhtinsky and his arguments, the Treaty of Kars was concluded between the Republic of Turkey on the one hand and the Azerbaijani, Georgian and Armenian SSRs on the other. Thus, this treaty became a full-fledged international legal document of regional significance. This far-sighted step bore fruit, which was skillfully used in the interests of Azerbaijan by the country's national leader Heydar Aliyev at the end of the XX century.

Perhaps the most controversial and unclear episode of the rich biography of Behbud Shahtakhtinsky can be called his death. For a long time, historical science was dominated by the viewpoint of his suicide, which many attributed to his unsuccessful personal life. At the same time, most researchers refer to the material about the death of B.Shahtakhtinsky in the issue of the newspaper "Shargin Sabahy" dated May 31, 1924. The newspaper reported: "Yesterday at 3 o'clock in the afternoon B.Shakhtakhtinsky shot himself with a firearm at his apartment in the house 25 on Kirpichnoe Lane. Tov. Shakhtakhtinsky came home at midday and locked himself in his room, and at 3 o'clock the neighbors heard four shots. Opening the door, they saw in the room fell on the bed with a nagan in his hand, half-naked. The whole bed was covered with blood. Despite the four shots to the head, he was still alive. B.Shakhtakhtinsky was immediately taken to the central hospital and died a short time later".

A careful analysis of this message reveals some inconsistencies. It is obvious that a person physically cannot shoot himself four times, moreover, in the head. This was pointed out by academician Isa Habibbeyli in his speech at the conference dedicated to the 130th anniversary of B. Shahtakhtinsky and the 90th anniversary of the Treaty of Kars. If we take into account the fact that the shots were fired from a nagan, which is not an automatic weapon and which requires pulling the trigger with force, the version of suicide seems even more doubtful. In addition, the nagan shoots through and through, i.e. its cartridges cannot get stuck in an obstacle. When shooting into the skull, two shots are more than enough for the brain to lose much of its function and the person to lose consciousness. Finally, the very thesis of suicide of such a strong-willed man as Behbud-aga Shahtakhtinsky seems unlikely. Thus, there is every reason to consider the version about terror - a favorite method of struggle with their opponents of both Bolsheviks and Bolshevized Dashnaks, who, most likely, could not forgive B.Shahtakhtinsky for his activities, which deprived them of the chance to seize the Nakhchivan region.

IBRAHIM ABILOV

History is not just a chain of events that happen in the course of time. History is a book of secrets, in which laws and norms are hidden to clarify the present and the future. Yes, these laws are hidden, but it is not to hide from the light of day, but in the name of preservation . Time passes, there comes a point when in order to understand present events one has to look back at the past and learn from it. Unfortunately, from time to time our historical memory falls into a kind of hibernation, and we forget how our enemies sowed discord between us. Over time, we often forgot even who our enemy was. The carriers of the pernicious Dashnak ideology poisoned our consciousness with poisonous seeds of suspicion towards ourselves. Ibrahim Abilov, a prominent Azerbaijani diplomat of the early 20th century, can serve as an example.

I.Abilov was born in 1882 in Ordubad. He entered the "Ekhtar" school opened by prominent Azerbaijani educator Magomed Tagi Sidgi, but the death of his father, which followed soon after, made Ibrahim need to help his family. He went to Petropavlovsk, which was then the name of present-day Makhachkala. Some time later Ibrahim came to Baku and started working as a laborer, and in 1903 he joined the leftist revolutionary movement. Soon he became an active member of the Azerbaijani social-democratic party "Hummet", established in 1904. In the ranks of this party he became a close associate of Nariman Narimanov. In 1907 I.Abilov was one of the organizers of the strike of sailors of Baku Caspian Trade Fleet. In 1912 he was for some time editor-in-chief of the newspaper "Baki Hayati". He was repeatedly arrested, and in 1913 was exiled to Astrakhan, where - here is a smile of Fortune! - just at that time N. Narimanov was a member of the city Duma. This coincidence was the starting point for a serious rapprochement between the two prominent figures of the Azerbaijani leftist movement. After the February Revolution, I.Abilov came to Tiflis, and at the end of the next year, 1918, he was elected a member of the parliament of the young Azerbaijan Democratic Republic, becoming a member of the Socialist faction.

After the Sovietization of Azerbaijan in 1920, Ibrahim Abilov was appointed Deputy Commissar of Internal Affairs of the Azerbaijan SSR. In September of the same year, at the 1st Congress of the Peoples of the East held in Baku, he was elected the first secretary of the Propaganda and Agitation Council of the Peoples of the East on the recommendation of N.Narimanov. On May 21, 1921 at the meeting of the Politburo and Orgburo of the Central Committee of the Communist Party of Azerbaijan I.Abilov together with G.Musabekov and M.Kahiani was elected to the delegation to the III Congress of Comintern. At the same time, the issue of sending him to Turkey as a representative of the Azerbaijan SSR was positively resolved in Moscow.

In August, I.Abilov arrived in Tiflis, and on September 21, in Batumi he boarded the Italian ship "Reno" bound for Istanbul. On his way he held meetings in a number of Turkish cities. I.Abilov met with prominent representatives of the Azerbaijani emigration, including the former head of the Counterintelligence Department of the Azerbaijan Democratic Republic Nagi Sheikhzamanli, military minister of the first government cabinet and then governor-general of Garabagh Khosrov-bek Sultanov, cavalry regiment commander Khosrov Mirza Bahman Kajar. On October 11, I.Abilov arrived in Ankara, and the next day he had a reception with Foreign Minister Yusuf Kemal. At this meeting, he achieved the solution of a number of important issues, including the opening of Azerbaijani consulates in the Black Sea cities of Trabzon and Samsun. On October 14, I.Abilov met with Mustafa Kemal Ataturk, founder of the Republic of Turkey, to whom he said the victories of the Turkish Liberation Army caused enthusiasm in Azerbaijan and the whole Muslim world. In response, Ataturk said: "Our nation is happy to hear the confirmation of this fact from the mouth of the representative of Azerbaijan. The people of Anatolia and Rumelia know that the hearts of Azerbaijanis beat in unison with them. The grief of

Azerbaijanis is our grief and their joy is our joy".

On October 22, I.Abilov presented his credentials to Ataturk. On November 18, a solemn flag-raising ceremony was held in Ankara over the post of the Azerbaijani SSR. M.Ataturk attended the ceremony.

Ibrahim Abilov conducted very fruitful diplomatic work in Turkey, and even managed to become one of Ataturk's closest friends, a friend of his family. M. Ataturk was among the participants of the banquet organized on the occasion of the birth of Ibrahim-Bek's second daughter, and even named her Anadolu and declared her his symbolic daughter. Thanks to I. Abilov's diplomatic activity, a number of bilateral and multilateral treaties were signed between Turkey and the Soviet republics. In 1921, at the Soviet-Turkish negotiations, I.Abilov together with the head of the Azerbaijani SSR delegation Behbud Shahtakhtinsky signed the Moscow and Kars Treaty, which laid the international legal foundation for the autonomy of the Nakhchivan region.

However, such a high level of Azerbaijani-Turkish relations, as it happened many times in different parts of history, clearly did not suit certain circles. In particular, this state of affairs alarmed Armenian nationalists, who had long served as a tool in the hands of the Russian Empire. This concern was clearly manifested in Baku and Moscow in December 1921, when the Azerbaijani representation in Ankara began to function. During this period, a campaign of purges of Muslim communists in the entourage of N. Narimanov began. The purge unleashed in the Baku City Party Committee was primarily directed against three prominent Azerbaijani diplomats - B.Shahtakhtinsky, A.Shirvani and I.Abilov.

Naturally, for I. Abilov, who had devoted his life to serving the revolution and the Soviet regime, the news of his expulsion from the Communist Party was a heavy blow. Seeing how the high ideals he had so enthusiastically served had become a bargaining chip in an unscrupulous political game, he reacted to this black ingratitude as sincerely and naturally as he had previously believed in and served revolutionary ideals. Here is what the secretary of the RSFSR Mission in Turkey Mikhailov wrote about it in a letter to G. Ordzhonikidze: "Seeing how this gray-haired party worker, suspended from the ranks of the party, sits and weeps, I called all the party formalists profanely".

Only after N. Narimanov's surety I. Abilov was restored to the Party ranks. After that

Narimanov said in a letter to Abilov: "Your line of behavior so far has been correct. I hope that you will not make mistakes in the future. We should not forget one thing: from the side of Russia and Turkey there are certain people who want to muddy the waters. Now it turns out that all counter-revolutionaries of the Transcaucasus have converged on this idea and want to turn the beautiful Caucasus into a sea of blood again".

Not shy in means, the enemies organized the poisoning of Ibragim Abilov at one of the receptions in Izmir, where he, as a diplomatic person, was supposed to be under guard. On his return from the banquet he felt sharp pains in his stomach and intestines. I. Abilov was operated by Ataturk's doctors, and he himself came to the hospital, not wanting to leave his friend alone. However, all the efforts of doctors were in vain, and I.Abilov died on February 23, 1923. His body was buried in Baku. The daughter of the Azerbaijani diplomat Anadolu-khanum remarked: "At that time it would not have occurred to anyone, but now it seems to me that my father may have been poisoned by Armenians. They did it, afraid of his influence and the successes he had achieved. They also wrote him anonymous letters..."

Yes, Ibragim Abilov had many detractors. After all, he achieved what others could not. He worked painstakingly and purposefully to strengthen Azerbaijani-Turkish friendship. It is known that history puts everything in its place. History has not preserved the names of those who made far-fetched accusations against Ibrahim Bey. On the other hand, after the beginning of the Great Patriotic War, both his daughters voluntarily went to the front; Anadolu Abilova reached Berlin as a nurse. Those who tried to use the fact of Abilov's poisoning in Turkey to sow the seeds of discord between the two brotherly nations did not achieve their dirty goals. After all, the people understood perfectly well who and for what purpose provoked fratricidal bloodshed since the wars between the state of Ak-Koyunlu and the Ottomans.

An eloquent fact: sworn enemies continued to take revenge on Ibragim Abilov even after his death. In one of her interviews his daughter Anadolu Abilova said: "After the war and returned to Baku with doctor Iskender Ismayilov, with whom we were married at the front. When we went to visit my father's grave, we found it destroyed and ruined .... Despite all the searches, we could not find his mummified remains, which were buried in an iron coffin. It seems that even Ibrahim Bey's grave frightened his foes. Be it not so. Who could have committed such barbarity but the Armenians!". In 1981, the grave of prominent statesman and diplomat Ibrahim Abilov was symbolically restored in the Alley of Honorable Burial in Baku by the order of Heydar Aliyev, the leader of Azerbaijan, the national leader of our people, who made the Azerbaijani-Turkish friendship firm and irreversible.

ZIYA YUSUF TALIBZADEH

Ziya Yusuf Talybzade is mentioned in sources mainly as a military commissar of the Nakhchivan Revolutionary Committee in 1921-1922. However, a number of authors point to his activities as the Commissar of Foreign Affairs.

Z.Y.Talibzade was born in 1877 in Tiflis and is the brother of the famous Azerbaijani playwright Abdulla Shaig. He received his elementary education in the school "Rushdiye" at the Transcaucasian Spiritual Administration, and higher spiritual education in the Iranian city of Mashhad. Having completed his education in Baghdad, Ziya Yusuf came to Baku in 1899. He was fluent in Arabic, Persian, Russian and Turkish.

In Baku, along with teaching, Z.Y.Talibzade engaged in literary activities and translations. In 1907, he went to Istanbul with an assignment from the famous philanthropist Haji Zeynalabdin Taghiyev to present a three-volume edition of the Koran in Azerbaijani to Sultan Abdulhamid II. Later, Ziya Yusuf was actively involved in political life. He received military education in Turkey, in the ranks of the Ottoman army participated in the Balkan War and the First World War on the Caucasian front, and in 1918 in the ranks of the Caucasian Islamic Army - in the liberation of Azerbaijan. He then headed the Ottoman diplomatic mission in Tabriz for some time.

In 1920 after the Sovietization of Azerbaijan Ziya Yusuf Talibzade was captured, but was released on the guarantee of Nariman Narimanov and with the experience of political and military work was appointed military commissar of Nakhchivan.

As it is known, on January 21, 1921 the Nakhchivan Regional Revolutionary Committee was established as a body of state power in this region, and in February Z.Y.Talibzadeh became its member. As a military commissar with the rank of general, he showed true valor in the defense of the region against the encroachments of Dashnak Armenia.

In October 1921, along with the Commissars of Food, Land, Finance, Health, Education, Internal and Military Affairs, the Commissars of Foreign Affairs, Communications, Labor, Internal and Foreign Trade, Social Security, Justice, the Extraordinary Commission, the Council of National Economy and the Military Tribunal were established as part of the Soviet People's Commissariat of the Nakhchivan SSR. The name of Akhund Yusuf Talibzade was mentioned for some time as the Commissar of Foreign Affairs.

In the book of Azerbaijani author H.Hasanov "National state views and activities of Nariman Narimanov" we read: "In 1920 he came to Azerbaijan at the request of N.Narimanov and was appointed as the Commissar of Foreign Affairs of Nakhchivan. His ties with Turkish pashas served to strengthen the security of Nakhchivan. Some time later, Akhund Yusuf (Ziya) Talibzade left Nakhchivan for Turkestan and together with Enver Pasha joined the Basmachi movement".

Apparently, his fluency in several foreign languages and his close ties in Turkey and Iran played a decisive role in the appointment of Yusuf Ziya Talybzadeh to the post of Commissar of Foreign Affairs. He honorably defended Nakhchivan from the Armenian Dashnaks, but could not reconcile himself with the liberalism and even flirtation of Bolshevik Russia with the Dashnaks.

At the end of 1922, Talybzade came to Baku and asked N. Narimanov for permission to leave the USSR. Having received the relevant document, he left for Central Asia and joined the Basmachi movement, becoming an associate of Enver Pasha. During that period he became close to the famous public and political figure Zeki Velidi Togan. During the struggle against the Bolsheviks, Ziya Yusuf Talibzade died.

GASYM-BEK JAMALBEKOV

Gasym-bek Jamalbekov, son of Abbasgulu bey Jamalbekov, was one of the diplomats who occupied a special place in the political history of Azerbaijan in the early 20th century. His life and socio-political activities were as controversial as the time itself, complex and ambiguous.

At the same time, thanks to his diplomatic gift and political sense, his ability to understand political peripetias, G.Jamalbekov managed to stay in the center of public and political events under the Russian Empire, under the Azerbaijan Democratic Republic and after Sovietization, defending the interests of Azerbaijan in the way he understood them and in the ways he considered right. Education was an important factor of his success in political and diplomatic activity. Born in 1881 in Nakhchivan, Gasym-bek was sent to a madrasa at the age of seven and then studied at the Nakhchivan "Mektebi Terbiye" ("School of Education"), which provided education in Azerbaijani, Russian and Persian languages. It should be noted that this school, opened in 1896, operated until the 30s, many representatives of Azerbaijani intelligentsia of that time studied there. Prominent poet and educator Magomed Tagi Sidgi taught Gasim-bek. Here young Gasim mastered Turkish and Persian languages perfectly, which played an important role in his later diplomatic career. After two years of study in "Mektebi Terbiye" he continued his studies in a four-year city school, and in 1901 he passed the exam at the Irevan Teachers' Seminary and received the title of a national teacher. Later Gasym-bek taught in various schools of Iravan province, and at the same time, under the influence of social-democratic ideas spreading during this period, he became involved in illegal political activities. In connection with the pogroms of Azerbaijani population by Armenian nationalists in 1905-1907, Gasym-bek returned to Nakhchivan. Gasym-bek returned to Nakhchivan and took an active part in the establishment of RSDLP cells in Nakhchivan and Julfa, and for some time he even headed the revision commission.

In 1912, G. Jamalbekov withdrew from teaching and joined the Julfa branch of an Iranian bank as a translator. A year later, he started working in another branch of the bank, in Iran. However, soon the main office of the bank received an order to get rid of Gasim-bek - apparently, information about his political activities reached the owners of the bank. Feeling the danger, Gasym-bek was going to come to Baku illegally, but was arrested and exiled to Krasnovodsk. However, according to researchers, after a short time he managed to escape and got to Baku, where with the help of a certain Jafar Akhundov he quietly settled in the territory of the mechanical plant "Rapid". The author of these lines found out that J.Akhundov was one of the founders of the first Marxist circle in Azerbaijan, a member of the social-democratic party "Hummet". At the time of adoption of the Declaration of Independence of Azerbaijan on May 28, 1918, Jafar Akhundov was a member of the Azerbaijan National Council, abstained from voting, thus becoming one of the two members of the Council who did not vote for the establishment of the Azerbaijani state.

After living illegally in Baku for several months, Gasym-bek was arrested again. But he again managed to escape arrest and reached Astrakhan by sea, where he found a prominent Azerbaijani diplomat, his fellow countryman Ibrahim Abilov, and found shelter with him.

After the establishment of the Azerbaijan Democratic Republic, H.Jamalbekov became a member of the parliament. Before that, he replaced Jafar Akhundov by entering the Azerbaijan National Council. The matter of his joining the council was discussed at the third session of the council on June 1, 1918 in Tiflis. G.Jamalbekov was a member of the National Council during the stay of the government of the republic in Ganja, as his name is mentioned in the resolution of June 17 on the composition of the second provisional government. Later, apparently, his negative attitude to the proclamation of the ADR led to his resignation from the Council.

In the ADR parliament, which opened on December 7, 1918, Gasym-bek

Jamalbekov was a member of the socialist faction, and a member of the central commission for the convocation of the Constituent Assembly. There was a 12-member "Muslim socialist faction" in the parliament headed by Aslan Safikurdsky, a deputy from Gazakh district, which included, along with other left-wing groups, representatives of the left wing of "Hummet" Samed Agamaly-oglu, Aligeydar Garayev, Ibrahim Abilov (Abilzade) and Gasym Dzhamalbekov.

After Sovietization, Gasym-bek was the first consul of the Nakhchivan SSR in the Iranian city of Tabriz. In the late 30s, G.Jamalbekov was among those who were subjected to political repression by the Soviet regime and was shot in Baku on January 9, 1938.

ISMAIL-BEK JAMALBEKOV

That was a very difficult and complicated period in the history of Nakhchivan region. In 1918-1920s, after the collapse of the huge Russian Empire, Nakhchivan, which was essentially cut off from the rest of Azerbaijan, faced its sworn enemy and fought steadfastly alone, both on the battlefield and in the diplomatic arena. It was a battle not only for Nakhchivan and not only for Azerbaijan, sometimes it even acquired religious, all-Muslim coloring. In 1915 in Nakhchivan and Julfa cities a nationalist party "Muja-Khidin", which means warriors for faith, was established. Four leaders of this party - Mirgeydarzade, I.Jamalbekov, K.Safarbekov and R.Safarbekov did a lot to repel the attacks of Armenian Dashnaks on Nakhchivan. Ismail Jamalbekov of them fought for Nakhchivan on diplomatic fronts and is worthy to enter the history of Azerbaijani diplomacy.

Ismail-bek Jamalbekov, son of Abbasgulu-bek Jamalbekov, was born in 1883 in Nakhchivan. In February 1918, when the Transcaucasian Sejm, which replaced the Transcaucasian Commissariat (the executive structure that replaced the Special Transcaucasian Committee on November 11, 1917), intensified its activities to form independent states in the region, I.Jamalbekov was in the first ranks of those who made efforts to establish a reliable defense of Nakhchivan region against Dashnak attacks, playing an important role in the formation of people's self-defense units. Due to his leadership qualities he gained great respect in a short time and became one of the leaders of the "Mujahidin" party. Later, in the 1920s, he was in diplomatic service as the first consul of the Nakhchivan SSR in the Iranian city of Maku.

S.Sadigov's book "From the History of the Nakhchivan Autonomous Republic" notes that in the 20s the Nakhchivan SSR had a wider autonomy, had its consulates in the Iranian cities of Maku, Khoy and Tabriz, its commissioner at the RSFSR consulate in the Turkish city of Kars, as well as representative offices in Baku, Tiflis and Iravan. In Nakhchivan itself, the military representation of Turkey operated until July 1924, and the Iranian consulate - until November 17, 1938. The first consuls of Nakhchivan were Ismail-bek Jamalbekov in Maku and Gasym-bek Jamalbekov in Tabriz. In January 1922, Aziz Sharif was appointed the representative of Nakhchivan SSR in the Georgian SSR.

It should be noted that Nakhchivan has long had close ties with Maku. In the spring of 1918, when Baku was in the hands of Dashnaks and SRs, the head of Nakhchivan National Committee Jafargulu Khan of Nakhchivan went to Maku Khanate, which was controlled by Ottoman troops at that time, and through the Khan negotiated with Turkish commanders about sending a military contingent to Nakhchivan. In a letter handed to Turkish commander Kyazim Karabekir on January 19, 1921, there are such lines: "The independence of Nakhchivan was recognized by the Soviet republics of Armenia, Ukraine, Dagestan, as well as the Khan of Maku and the head of the city of Tabriz."

In January 1921, a mutiny broke out among the officers of the 106th regiment of the XI Red Army, stationed in the Nakhchivan village of Shakhtakhty. On the night of January 11, despite the measures taken by the emergency commissariat and the Turkish command, almost 300 soldiers and officers of the regiment crossed the bridge over the Araz River into the territory of the Makin Khanate. This incident led to tension between the Nakhchivan SSR and the Khanate. Murtuzagulu Khan was dissatisfied with the fact that the rebellious Red Army soldiers, having joined Denikin's forces on Iranian territory, began to engage in robbery and plunder, and broke off relations with Nakhchivan. Ismail-Bek Jamalbekov played a significant role in normalization of bilateral relations. When he was consul in Maku, he staunchly defended the interests of Nakhchivan and Azerbaijan as a whole.

It is possible that his integrity and devotion to national interests attracted the unfriendly attention of the Soviet authorities and, at the same time, the Dashnaks disguised as Bolsheviks. On January 5, 1938, the visiting session of the military board of the Supreme Court of the USSR sentenced Ismail-Bek for "counter-revolutionary-nationalist activity" to execution by firing squad. The sentence was carried out the next day. Ismail Jamalbekov's wife Gullu Sharif-kyzy as "wife of a traitor of the motherland" was arrested on December 31, 1937 in accordance with the decision of the CEC of the USSR of July 4, 1934 and sentenced to 8 years of correctional labor camps by the decision of the Special Conference of the NKVD of the USSR of April 9, 1938.

BALABEK ALIBEKOV

In the process of collecting information about diplomats of the past - natives of the Nakhchivan region, my attention was drawn to one name mentioned in Said Sadigov's book "From the History of the Nakhchivan Autonomous Republic" (1995), as well as by several authors referring to this work. This is one Balabek, who held the post of the Nakhchivan SSR Commissioner in Kars in the 1920s. None of these authors gives the surname of this person or information about his identity. However, a number of other works, which contain data on the history of the museum business in Nakhchivan, mention a certain Balabek Alibekov, the creator of the first museum in this city. Our comparisons showed that it was Balabek Alibekov who worked as a commissioner in Kars for some time.

It should be noted that unlike the cities of Maku, Khoy and Tabriz, there was not a consulate of the Nakhchivan SSR in Kars, but an authorized representative at the RSFSR consulate. On February 7, 1924, notes were exchanged in Ankara regarding consular organizations between Turkey and the USSR, after which Soviet consulates were opened in Istanbul, Izmir, Kars, Artvin, Erzerum and Trabzon. The last four Soviet consulates were closed in February 1938.

To date, the most concrete among the known information that Balabek Alibekov was the NSSR commissioner in Kars is Ferman Khalilov's book "Scientific Society for the Study of Nakhchivan". Gathering data about Nakhchivan museum, the author turned to the honored teacher of Azerbaijan Lyatif Huseynzade: ".... Knowing B.Alibekov well, candidate of philological sciences L.Huseynzadeh during a conversation with us in June 2005 remembered that B.Alibekov worked in the embassy (consulate) in Kars on some position and had good ties with Kars". In addition, research on the museum opened by B.Alibekov was also conducted by Nizami Rahimov, director of the Nakhchivan State Museum of History, who gave valuable information about his museum activities.

As a result of our searches it turned out that Balabek Alibekov was born in 1855 in Nakhchivan. The matter is that in the 6th protocol of the special commission for the study of Nakhchivan region dated April 4, 1925 it is stated that Balabek Alibekov is 70 years old. In 1903-1908 he served as a police officer, in 1908-1911 - as an interpreter in the police department of Kars. - As an interpreter in the police department of Kars. In 1911 he retired, but his extensive experience and good command of Russian, Persian and Turkish languages, as well as his authority among the local population led to the fact that B.Alibekov was retained in the service and in 1911-1917 worked in the police department as an interpreter. From 1917 to 1920, he held the position of police chief in Urmiye. Later he worked in Soviet institutions, and from March-April 1924 to the beginning of 1925 he held the post of Nakhchivan SSR Commissioner in Kars, which he knew for a long time. We do not know the exact time when he left this post, but it is clear that in April 1925 Balabek Alibekov was no longer employed in diplomatic work: the above-mentioned 6th protocol of the special commission of April 4, 1925 states that he was tried as a financial agent of the Commissariat of Finance of the Nakhchivan SSR and eventually dismissed.

Balabek Alibekov came from an ancient Bek family. He was also a famous collector, collecting various items related to the history, culture and ethnography of the Nakhchivan region. In 1917-1918 he arranged a museum in his house located in the center of Nakhchivan city - this fact eloquently testifies to his deep interest in history and culture. In the article "Balabek Alibekov's Nakhchivan Museum" by Nizami Rahimov, it is noted that this house was located in the place where later, up to the last years, there was a communal and household combine.

It should be noted that the museum created by B.Alibekov as a private initiative played a significant role in his fate after his dismissal from the NSSR Finance Ministry in April 1925. After the resolution of the sovnarkom of the Nakhchivan ASSR of October 30, 1924 on the establishment of the Nakhchivan Historical-Ethnographic Museum remained unfulfilled, the private museum of B.Alibekov was officially transferred to the republican property by the resolution of the same sovnarkom of January 6, 1926, and Balabek Alibekov himself was appointed director for life with a salary of 40 rubles. B.Alibekov was also mentioned as the director of the museum in the protocol #33 of the Scientific Society for the Study of Nakhchivan dated February 12, 1927.

It can be assumed that Balabek Alibekov died around 1940s.

So, in the 20s of XX century Balabek Alibekov, a skillful diplomat and at the same time one of the founders of the museum business in the Nakhchivan region of

Azerbaijan, worked at the RSFSR Consulate in Kars as an authorized representative of the Nakhchivan SSR.

RZA TAHMASIB

"No matter what difficulties you encounter in life, never lose your objectivity and principle^" - this phrase of Rza Tahmasib, a prominent figure of Azerbaijani theater and cinema, participant in the creation of 17 popular feature films, from his memoirs "Unforgettable" not only reflects his life credo, but can also be perceived as a concise statement of the principle of his diplomatic activity.

When I read this Tahmasib phrase, I was reminded of a statement by one of the characters in the novel The Diplomat by the writer James Aldridge: "Diplomacy needs people who are enlightened and accustomed to objectivity."

In-depth study of the diplomatic activity of Rza Tahmasib (Rza-bek Tahmasibbekov) requires extensive painstaking work in the archives of Russia and Turkey. So far, we only know that this outstanding man, who lived a complex and rich 86-year life, worked at the diplomatic mission of Azerbaijan SSR in Turkey for about a year. This year was a difficult period in the history of both Azerbaijan and Turkey. R.Tahmasib was entrusted with diplomatic tasks at such a difficult time due to his broad outlook, education, high prestige in the society, and not least his fluent command of Russian, Arabic, Persian and Turkish languages.

In 1901, Rza-bek entered the "Mektebi Terbiye" ("School of Education") opened in Nakhchivan by prominent Azerbaijani educator and poet Magomed Tagi

Sidgi. Russian, Arabic and Persian languages, history and geography were taught here. Having studied in this school for 5 years, he entered a three-class city school, from which he graduated in 1909.

The beginning of Rza Tahmasib's active socio-political activity falls on 1917-1918, when Nakhchivan district turned into an arena of confrontation between imperialist powers. During this period, Armenian Dashnaks carried out bloody ethnic cleansing of the Azerbaijani population throughout the region. Under the influence of the bourgeois revolution in Russia, crowded rallies were held in Nakhchivan, one of the organizers and active participants of which was R.Tahmasib. Later, in the spring and summer of 1918, when the entire region was engulfed by tragic events, when the Dashnaks committed bloody excesses in the villages of Negram, Shakhtakhty and a number of others, Rza-bek fought bravely in the ranks of self-defense units formed by the residents of the region and participated in the defense of Nakhchivan.

After 1918 R. Tahmasib lived in Baku, where he also actively participated in social and political life. In 1921, after Sovietization, he received an offer to work as an interpreter at the diplomatic mission of the Azerbaijan SSR in Turkey. In September, the Azerbaijani delegation of 28 people, among whom was Rza-bek, departed from Tiflis to Batum, where they loaded on the Italian steamer "Reno" going to Istanbul. The State Archive of Azerbaijan keeps the document "Composition of the Plenipotentiary Representation of the Azerbaijan SSR in Ankara and table of monthly salaries", from which it follows that R.Tahmasib was an employee of the information department. It should be noted that Rza-Bek became one of the closest assistants of the first Azerbaijani SSR Plenipotentiary Representative in Turkey Ibrahim Abilov. At the same time, he was actively interested in the cultural life of Turkey. Rza Tahmasib was the inspirer and organizer of the predominant majority of charitable events held by the Azerbaijani postpresidency. Azerbaijani researcher Fergana Huseynova's book "Cultural aspects of Azerbaijani-Turkish relations in the period of independence (science, education, culture)" gives information about some theater performances and other cultural events held by the post office on the basis of archival materials. From one of such documents.

"The program of the Azerbaijani evening" reveals that Rza Tahmasib took on the functions of the director of the arranged performance and in addition played two roles in it.

On February 17, 2013, "Respublika" newspaper published an article by Tarana Jabiyeva on the history of Azerbaijani diplomacy, in which, in particular, we read: "Employees of the Azerbaijani embassy headed by Ibrahim Abilov also held charitable events to provide material assistance to orphans and at the same time to promote the rich culture of Azerbaijan in Turkey. In those years, "Ashug Garib" opera was staged by the Embassy staff. Nadir Ibrahimov, Asker Topchibashev, Ismail Ismayilov, Mirza Davud Rasulzade masterfully coped with roles in this production. At concerts I.Abilov paid much attention to playing tara, kamancha, whistle. A.Khakverdiev's play "The Unfortunate Young Man", directed by Rza Tahmasib, was staged at charity evenings.

According to historical data, R. Tahmasib returned to his homeland in August 1922, that is, before the death of I. Abilov, and further devoted his life to the development of the national theater art and cinema.

While working on this article, the author's attention was drawn to two cases from the subsequent biography of Rza Tahmasib, which testify to his great courage and at the same time wit.

In the 1930s, when political persecution and repression were intensifying in the country, Rza-bek returned home one evening excited. He quickly changed his clothes and hurried to an important meeting, of which he had been notified too late. However, he was late and entered the hall when everyone was already seated. When he saw him, the secretary of the Central Committee Mirjafar Bagirov asked him in an irritated tone:

- Are you Rosa Tazmasian?

Those present laughed at this remark of "himself". Rza-bek did not understand anything and at first was embarrassed, but then he noticed a telegram in Bagirov's hands.

- Comrade Bagirov, the telegram must be from an Armenian.

Bagirov's face turned sour, and silence reigned in the hall. After the meeting, Rza-bek learned that the telegram had come from a Bulgarian film studio.

Another case, which testifies to the uncommon courage of Rza Tahmasib for those times, is related to the shooting of the famous movie "Arshin Mal Alan". Rza-bek chose for shooting of one of the episodes the dacha of not anyone but chairman of Azerbaijan's KGB Emelyanov in Shuvalan village and sent him a letter about it. The answer was positive: according to literary sources, Emelyanov received R.Tahmasib, listened to him and gave permission for filming. When Rza-bek was leaving his office, Emelyanov said: "If the movie does not turn out, blame yourself." Not surprisingly, this threatening remark echoed in his ears for a long time - until the end of filming.

By the way, it was very difficult to watch the movie. The film was accepted after much controversy, but brought a group of members of the creative team, including R. Tahmasib, the State Prize.

In conclusion, we have to state that the socio-political and diplomatic activity of Rza Tahmasib, known for his services to Azerbaijani theater and cinema, is still waiting for a comprehensive researcher.

AZIZ SHARIF

The Nakhchivan region of Azerbaijan has historically maintained close ties with Georgian states. Thus, according to historical sources, the founder of Nakhchivan Khanate Heydargulu Khan concluded a military alliance with Kartli - Kakheti kingdom. In the middle of the 18th century, political and cultural ties between Nakhchivan and Adjara were noticeably revitalized.

The 1916 documents contain information about the active participation of Azerbaijani writer Ali Sabri Gasimov, a native of Nakhchivan, in the activities of the Batumi Muslim Charity Society. In his memoirs, the writer points out that the society operated on the territory from Batum to Trabzon, providing assistance to Muslim refugees. Alekper Gharib, a poet from Nakhchivan, was also a member of this society. Besides, as it is found out from sources, during the mentioned period in Batumi and Ardagan, Colonel Ibragim-bek Gadimov, a native of Nakhchivan, actively defended the interests of peaceful Muslims who suffered from violence and arbitrariness. At the end of XIX - beginning of XX century millionaire from Nakhchivan Mirza Heydar Nasirbekov maintained close trade ties with Batum. Part of the needs of Batumi district in cotton was covered by Nakhchivan district. At the same time, various goods from Nakhchivan district traveled through Batum to Trabzon and further to European markets. These connections were preserved to a greater or lesser extent after the Sovietization of Azerbaijan.

In the 1920s-1924s, the Nakhchivan SSR had its representative offices in Iran, Turkey and the Soviet republics of Georgia and Armenia. Said Sadygov's book "From the History of the Nakhchivan Autonomous Republic" reports that in the 1920s, the Nakhchivan SSR had post-representations in Baku, Tiflis and Iravan. In January 1922 Aziz Sharif, a prominent critic, literary critic and translator, was appointed the representative of this republic in Georgia. He was born on March 28, 1895 in Nakhchivan, graduated from "Mektebi Terbiye" ("School of Education") of the famous Azerbaijani educator Magomed Tagi Sidgi, partially mastering Persian and Russian languages. Then he continued his studies at the boarding school opened in Tiflis by prominent Azerbaijani writer and publicist Jalil Mammadguluzade. After the closure of this school, he lived in a certain Russian family, where he learned Russian and French languages well. In his memoirs "From Days of the Past" Aziz Sharif says: "When the boarding school in Tiflis was closed, my father on the advice and with the help of Mirza (J.Mammadguluzade - ed.) entrusted me to a Russian family. This family consisted of three women, and their house was located on Mikhailovskaya Street, near the Mujtehid Square. In this house an elderly woman lived with her two teacher daughters. ...In the house they spoke to me in Russian and French. I remember that during this time I learned to speak both of these languages fluently, as well as to read and write in them.

A.Sharif's notes also show that he lived in Tiflis until spring 1906, when he was forced to return to his native Nakhchivan, where bloody excesses against the peaceful Azerbaijani population were also taking place due to the Armenian-Muslim massacres that broke out at the instigation of the tsarist regime. Then he studied for some time in the Irevan Boarding School opened by Ibadulla-bey Muganli and Jabbar-bey Mammadov, and in 1908 he began to study in Tiflis again. In 1915-1917 he studied at the Moscow Commercial Institute. As a result, he became well versed in French, Russian, Persian and Georgian languages.

By the end of the First World War, the political situation in the Caucasus was extremely tense. In 1917, Aziz Sharif returned to Nakhchivan, where he did much to eliminate anarchy and lawlessness. Fakhreddin Jalilov's book "Nakhchivan District Police (1820-1920)", based on archival documents, reports that in late 1917, Aziz Sharif formed a workers' and peasants' "Red Guard" in the district.

In January 1918 he was elected Chairman of the Soviet of Workers' and Soldiers' Deputies. A.Sharif sent a number of letters to the Transcaucasian Commissariat on ways to stabilize the situation in Nakhchivan, and he himself went to Tiflis to present the situation to the heads of the Commissariat.

In the 20s and 30s, Aziz Sharif lived in Tiflis, practicing journalism and publishing. In all probability, his good knowledge of the Tiflis environment and extensive ties with the local intelligentsia, as well as his fluency in several languages played a decisive role in assigning him the duties of the representative of the Nakhchivan SSR in the Georgian SSR. It should be recalled that during this period the Nakhchivan SSR was represented in Tabriz by Gasym-bek Jamalbekov, in Maku by Ismail-bek Jamalbekov, and in Kars by Balabek Alibekov.

From the history of diplomacy

NAKHCHIVAN IN DIPLOMATIC ACTIVITIES AND THE WORK OF ABBASGULU AGA BAKIKHANOV

Abbasgulu Aga Bakikhanov lived in one of the most difficult periods of Azerbaijan's history. He is among the most prominent personalities of Azerbaijan in the XIX century. His reputation as the father of Azerbaijani historical science was firmly established. In other words, Abbasgulu aga Bakikhanov for
Herodotus is of the same importance for Azerbaijani historical science as Herodotus is for the world science, and his fundamental historical work "Gulustani" is of the same importance for the world science.
Irem" ("Paradise Flower Garden") - which is what Herodotus's Hist.

Abbasgulu aga Bakikhanov is recognized as one of the three first Azerbaijani educators. Such works as "Ganuni-Gudsi" ("Sacred Law"), "Esrar ul-melekut" ("Secrets of the Kingdom of Heaven"), "Tehzibul-ekhlag" ("Moral Purity"), "Ein ul-mizan" ("Essence of Scales") recommend him as having encyclopedic knowledge in linguistics, astronomy, geography, logic, psychology and other disciplines. Being a poet, enlightener and historian at the same time, A.Bakikhanov can be called the Voltaire of Azerbaijani enlightenment. Along with this, he was also an outstanding diplomat and was able to give a profound assessment of contemporary events and processes and, caring for the good of the Motherland, served its interests at crucial moments of history.

It should be pointed out that Nakhchivan occupies a special place in both diplomatic and scientific-historical activities of A. Bakikhanov. On December 20, 1819 at the invitation of General Yermolov Abbasgulu agha Bakikhanov came to Tiflis, where he was accepted to the Main Military Administration in the Caucasus as an interpreter of Oriental languages and worked there for almost 26 years. On September 4, 1820 Abbasgulu aga was promoted to warrant officer, on July 20, 1826 - to lieutenant, on October 14, 1827 - to staff captain, on August 7, 1828 - to captain, on April 21, 1829 - to major, on March 9, 1832 he became lieutenant colonel.

One of the most important tasks assigned to Abbasgulu agha Bakikhanov in the military-diplomatic service was the resolution of border disputes at the conclusion of the Gulustan peace agreement of 1813 between Russia and Iran. A little later Abbasgulu agha took part in the war of 1826-1828 for Nakhchivan and Irevan khanates. He fought in all the battles in the vicinity of Nakhchivan, and was awarded the rank of staff captain for his services in the capture by Russian troops of the fortress of Abbasabad, located on the bank of the Araz River, 6 km southeast of the city of Nakhchivan. This fortress was built in 1809-1810 according to the project of French military advisors and was considered one of the most impregnable bastions of that time. As noted in the "Encyclopedia of Monuments of Nakhchivan", the Abbasabad fortress played an important role in the defense of Iranian positions. Some authors believe that A.Bakikhanov took part in the negotiations of the Russian command with the commandant of Abbasabad fortress Ehsan Khan Kengerli. By the way, one of the descendants of the enlightener and poet, Gultekin Bakikhanova, reports about it in her book "Etudes about Gudsi" (1984).

In Enver Akhmedov's book "Abbasgulu Aga Bakikhanov: Epoch, Life, Activity" (1989), Russian General Paskevich assessed his diplomatic talent: "In the war with Persia, I especially rely on his military activity". The general further draws attention to the fact that due to A. Bakikhanov's diplomatic talent, his deep understanding of the current events and his fluent command of Farsi, all diplomatic negotiations with Persia were mediated by him.

The official portal of Nakhchivan AR posted the following material:

"Bakikhanov and A.S.Griboyedov on their way to Iran stopped to stay at the palace of Ehsan khan Kengerli. A.S.Griboyedov mentions about it in his travel notes "Erivan campaign". According to Azerbaijani historian Musa Guliyev, in 1828 A.Bakikhanov spent more than four months in Nakhchivan and wrote letters in Russian to his wife Sakina khanim from the neighboring village Garabaglar. These letters were later translated and published in the magazine "Azerbaijan" - the organ of the Union of Writers of Azerbaijan.

Abbasgulu aga Bakikhanov's fundamental work "Gulistani-Irem" is one of the most important sources on the history of not only the Caucasus as a whole, but also the Nakhchivan region. The book mentions events related to the cities of Nakhchivan, Julakh (Julfa), Nakhchivan salt mines, Alynjak (Alinje) fortress, Sharur and Ordubad. It seems to the authors of these lines that the following passage in the mentioned work is of fundamental importance from the point of view of historical geography of Nakhchivan region: "At the end of Nadir's time Panah bey Ibrahim Halil oglu Javanshir fled and hid in Sheki and Shirvan country and after long wars raised the banner of his khan's power in Karabakh. He built first Bayat fortress and then Tarnaut. He seized lands from Khudaferin bridge to the river Kurokchay and Bergushad district. In addition, he occupied the districts of Meghri and Guney belonging to Garadagh, Tatif and Sisyan belonging to Nakhchivan, Terter-Kolany belonging to Erivan, Zangezur and Kapan belonging to Tabriz. At times he also subjugated Ardabil and other neighboring countries".

As we can see, at one time Tatif and Sisian, which today are part of Armenia, were part of the Azerbaijani Nakhchivan Khanate. The book contains many equally valuable and topical facts on the history of Azerbaijan in general and Nakhchivan in particular.

NAKHCHIVAN'S PLACE IN AZERBAIJANI-POLISH RELATIONS

Today, Nakhchivan occupies a prominent place in Azerbaijani-Polish ties. The positive dynamics of development of these ties gives grounds for confidence that cooperation between the regions of the two countries will be an important support for strengthening relations between the two countries.

The history of Azerbaijani-Polish relations dates back to the Middle Ages. The Azerbaijani state of Ak-Koyunlu, which emerged in the XV century, established diplomatic relations with Poland. In 1470, the ruler of Ak-Koyunlu Uzun-Gasan sent his envoy Murad and Venetian ambassador Lazaro Quirino, who was in Tabriz, to negotiate with Venice, Pope Paul II and Poland on an alliance against the Ottoman Empire. According to historian Ya.Mahmudov, after some time Uzun Hasan, seeing that there was no news from the envoys, sent another envoy to Europe, who held negotiations with the Polish king, and then together with his envoy went to Venice, from where they returned to Tabriz. It is also known that in 1473-1478, Uzun-Hasan sent another envoy to Europe. Uzun-Hasan sent his diplomats to the Polish court and negotiated on various issues.

These ties were preserved under the Safavids as well. Thus, Safavid Shah Abbas I sent an embassy to Europe headed by famous diplomat Oruj Beyat, authorizing him to hold negotiations with Russia, Poland and 8 other states. One of the most interesting documents concerning Azerbaijani-Polish relations is a letter of Shah Sultan Huseyn (1694-1722) to Prince of Saxony and King of Poland Friedrich August. Besides, this letter is considered one of the first diplomatic documents written in Azerbaijani language. This is reported in the article "Two letters of Iranian Shahs in Turkish" by Dr. Lajos Fekete, published in 1934 in Turkey.

The second half of the 19th - early 20th centuries was marked by a noticeable revival of Azerbaijani-Polish relations, and this is not accidental: both countries were part of the Russian Empire. During this period, contacts were established between orientalist scientists, military men and diplomats. A notable event in this context is the appointment in 1839 of the cavalry general Ismail-Khan of Nakhchivan as naib of the Transcaucasian Muslim cavalry regiment stationed in Warsaw. The next year Ismail-khan, having distinguished himself at maneuvers near Warsaw, was promoted to ensign, and in 1844 - to staff-captain. It should be noted that in 2010 in the journal "Scientific Notes" of Nakhchivan State University was published an article by historian Musa Guliyev "About Kengerlin horsemen who went from Nakhchivan to Warsaw". The article contains valuable information about the units of the Kengerli cavalry sent from Nakhchivan to Warsaw in the 40s of the XIX century, with the main attention paid to the military uniform of Azerbaijani cavalrymen.

Various historical sources contain data that during the mentioned period in the Transcaucasian Muslim Cavalry Regiment in Warsaw served officers of the Kengerli cavalry - Capt. Huseyn Sultan, Hasan-aga Nazar sultan-ogly, Colonel Ismail-aga Kengerli, Iskender-aga Novruz-aga oglu, Almurad-bek Mamedgulu sultan-ogly, Najafgulu-aga Kengerli and Rzagulu-aga Kengerli. It is not excluded that this list is incomplete, and in the future the names of other Azerbaijani officers - natives of the Nakhchivan region who served on Polish soil may be revealed.

On the other hand, Polish travelers, diplomats and writers visited Nakhchivan at different times. Among them, it is worth mentioning the Russian writer, orientalist and diplomat of Polish nationality Alexander Chodzko Boreyko, who was the Russian consul in Persia in the 1930s and visited Nakhchivan along the way. Khodzko collected information about the culture, including folklore and oral literature of the peoples of the East, including Azerbaijanis. As a student in St. Petersburg, he studied Oriental languages with Mirza Jafar Topchibashev, and in 1842 translated the Azerbaijani version of the Koroglu epic into English and published it in London.

The authors of these lines spoke in the press about attempts to "Armenianize" a postage stamp depicting a battle scene from the Russian-Japanese War of 1904-1905, among the persons depicted on which is a prominent Azerbaijani military commander Huseyn-Khan Nakhchivan. It should be noted that the image of this scene belongs to Victor Mazurovsky (18591917), a representative of one of the noble Polish families.

On the eve of the collapse of the Russian Empire in the Russian Duma, the Pole Ledinsky and the Azerbaijani Topchibashev fought for the autonomy of their countries. After World War I, thousands of Poles deported from their homeland found refuge in Azerbaijan.

Speaking about the origins of Azerbaijani Polish ties, national leader of the

Azerbaijani people Heydar Aliyev said: "Azerbaijan's ties with Poland have a long history. Back in the 19th century, revolutionaries exiled from Poland for their political views found a second homeland in Azerbaijan. The role of Poles - specialists and scientists - in the development of Baku oil industry since the second half of the XIX century is significant. Engineer V.Zglenitsky, geologist K.Bogdanovich and others contributed to the industrial oil production in Azerbaijan. During this period, Azerbaijani oil producers turned to Polish engineers and architects for construction works. Dozens of buildings in Baku today, preserved from the past centuries, were erected by Polish architects".

On October 1, 1919, Magomed-khan Tekinsky, a well-known diplomat born in Nakhchivan, was appointed Deputy Minister of Foreign Affairs of the Azerbaijan Democratic Republic and headed the negotiations held in Baku with Waclaw Ostrovsky, the Polish representative in the Caucasus.

After the fall of the Azerbaijan Democratic Republic, the activity of Azerbaijani political migrants in neighboring Turkey, of course, never met the interests of the USSR. Therefore, since 1930 Azerbaijani political migrants had to go to a new emigration once again. At this difficult moment, many of them were sheltered by Poland.

The authors of these lines also studied the history of Nakhchivan's cultural ties with Poland. In 1984, the Azerbaijani folk dance ensemble of yalla "Sharur" participated in the decade of Azerbaijani culture and art in Poland.

Poland recognized Azerbaijan's independence on December 27, 1991, and diplomatic relations between the two countries were established on February 21, 1992. But the real development of bilateral relations is connected with the name of Heydar Aliyev. On August 26-28, 1997, President of Azerbaijan Heydar Aliyev visited Poland at the invitation of President of the Republic Alexander Kwasniewski. In 2001, the Embassy of Poland in Azerbaijan was opened, and in 2004, the Embassy of Azerbaijan in Poland was opened.

It should be noted that Nakhchivan also occupies a prominent place in the Azerbaijani-Polish relations of the modern era. In 2010, Polish Ambassador Krzysztof Krajewski visited Nakhchivan and had a conversation with Chairman of the Supreme Majlis of the Nakhchivan Autonomous Republic Vasif Talibov. The parties expressed satisfaction with the establishment of ties between Poland and Nakhchivan Autonomous Republic during K.Krajewski's term of office. In September 2011, K.Krajewski's successor as Polish Ambassador to Azerbaijan Michal Labenda visited Nakhchivan and was also received by Chairman of the Supreme Majlis V.Talibov. Prospects of establishing ties between Nakhchivan AR and various regions of Poland, first of all in the field of science and culture, agriculture were discussed at the meeting. In 2012, the Ambassador together with the Rector of the General Trade School of Poland Adam Budnikowski visited Nakhchivan again. At the meeting held at Nakhchivan State University, an agreement on inter-university exchange was signed.

In September 2011, the founding conference of the Annual Conference of Regional and Local Authorities of the Eastern Partnership Countries (CORLEAP), which was established within the framework of the Eastern Partnership Program of the European Union (EC), was held in Poznan. Nakhchivan Autonomous Republic participated in this conference at the invitation of the European Committee of Regions and became a founding member of the new organization. Since February 2012 Nakhchivan Autonomous Republic has been a member of CORLEAP bureau.

In 2013, as a result of cooperation between the Supreme Majlis of Nakhchivan Autonomous Republic and the Embassy of Poland in Azerbaijan, commemorative medals of historical monuments in the territory of the autonomy were produced. The medals depict the mausoleums of Momine Khatyn, Yusuf Kuseyir oglu, Karabaglar, Prophet Noah and Huseyn Javid.

As can be seen from the above, today Nakhchivan occupies a prominent place in Azerbaijani-Polish ties. The positive dynamics of development of these ties gives grounds for confidence that cooperation between the regions of the two countries will be an important support for strengthening relations between the two countries.

REFERENCE

1. 1913-1916-ci illarda Rusiyanin "Harbi tarix jurnali"
2. 1937-38-da gullalananan (habs olunan) §axslar - (alava 570 adam) Tartibgi:

   Q. Tahirzada (www.adam.az "Yadda§in barpasi" maqalasi, 1 ("Sarhad" qazetininin xususi buraxili§i)
3. Aleksandr Xodzko maqalasi, www.az.wikipedia.org/Aleksandr_ Xodzko, istifada tarixi: 09.03.2013-cu il
4. Atnur i.E.. Osmanli idaragiliyindan sovet idaragiliyina qadar Naxgivan (19181920), Naxgivan: 0cami, 2013, 496 s.
5. Azarbaycan Respublikasi Prezidenti adindan Pol§a Respublikasinin Prezidenti Aleksandr Kvasnevskinin §arafina ta§kil olunmu§ rasmi qabulda Heydar Qliyevin nitqi (Baki, 27 oktyabr 1999-cu il) sanadina tarixi arayi§
6. Azarbaycan - Pol§a munasibatlari, 5 aprel 2010-cu il tarixda tartib olunmu§ umumi tarixi arayi§, "Heydar Qliyev irsi" Beynalxalq elektron kitabxanasininin internet sayti - www.lib.aliyev-heritage.org
7. Azarbaycan Xalq Cumhuriyyati (1918-1920) Parlament (Stenoqrafik hesabatlar), I cild, Baki, 1998, 976 s.
8. Azarbaycan Xalq Cumhuriyyati Ensiklopediyasi, iki cildda I cild, Baki: Lider, 2004, 440 s.
9. Azarbaycan Xalq Cumhuriyyati Ensiklopediyasi. iki cildda. II cild. Baki: Lider, 2005,472 s.
10. Azarbaycan Kommunist Partiyasinin tarixi, Baki, 1979, 423 s.
11. Azarbaycan Respublikasi Prezidentinin i§lar idarasi, Siyasi Sanadlar arxivi, Fond 268, siyahi 23, i§. 196, v. 11
12. Azarbaycan tarixi. Yeddi cildda. V cild (1900-1920-ci illar). Baki: Elm. 2008. 696 s.
13. Cabiyeva T. Diplomatiya tariximizdan // "Respublika" qazeti, 17 fevral 2013-cu il, No. 037, s. 5.
14. Cafarov F. Naxgivan Qaza polisi (1828-1920-ci illar), Baki: Nurlan, 2008, 192 s.

15. Oliyev N. Oli Sabri Qasimov - unudulmaqda olan diplomat, doyu§gu, yazigi // 525-ci qazet, 2010, 2 fevral. s.6.
16. Gorkamli saxsiyyatlar maqalasi. www.nakhchivan.az
17. Gumru, Moskva va Qars muqavilalalari va Naxgivanin taleyi (Tartibgi va on soz muallifi i.Haciyev) Baki, 1999, 138 s.
18. Haciyev A. Qars va Araz-Turk respublikalarinin tarixindan. Baki: Azarnasr, 1994, 124 s.
19. Haciyev I. Azarbaycan Xalq Cumhuriyyati va Naxgivan. Naxgivan: Ocami, 2010, 384 sah.
20. Haciyev I. Behbud aga Sahtaxtinski: Naxgivanin arazi masalasi va muxtariyyat statusu // "Naxgivan" ictimai-siyasi, adabi-badii, elmi-publisistik jurnal, No. 23, Naxgivan: Ocami, 2011, 207 s.
21. Haciyev I. Behbud aga Sahtaxtinski. Naxgivan: Ocami, 2016, 80 s.
22. Haciyev I. Naxgivan Muxtar Respublikasininin yaranmasi: tarix va muasirlik // AMEA NB "Xabarlar" jurnali, Naxgivan, 2009, No. 19, s. 21-34
23. Habibbayli I. Behbud aga Sahtaxtinskinin siyasi faaliyyati va taleyi // "Naxgivan" ictimai-siyasi, adabi-badii, elmi-publisistik jurnal, №23, Naxgivan: Ocami, 2011, 207 s.
24. Habibbayli I. Mahammadaga Sahtaxtli taleyi va sanati. Baki: Nurlan, 2008, 166 s.
25. Hasanov H. Nariman Narimanovun milli dovlatgilik baxislari va faaliyyati. Baki, 2005, 248 s.
26. Hasimli H. Oli Sabri. Baki: Nurlan.2007, 141 s.
27. Huseynova F. "Mustaqillik dovrunda Azarbaycan Turkiya alaqalarinin kulturoloji aspektlari (elm, tahsil, madaniyyat)". Baki, 2007, 302 s.
28. Xalilov F. Naxgivani oyranan elmi camiyyat, Baki: Nurlan, 2005, 196 s.
29. ivanov R. Basqin (Bolseviklarin sovet torpagi qadim Naxgivanda azginliqlari haqda aci haqiqatlar). Naxgivan, 2013, 463 s.
30. Kalbizada E. Axal-Taki vadisindan Araz vadisina // "Sarq qapisi" qazeti, 29 noyabr 2013-cu il, No. 224, s.3
31. Kalbizada E. Daha bir saxta ermani tabligati // "Sarq qapisi" qazeti, 243 (20.897), 26 dekabr 2013-cu il, s. 4.

32. Kalbizada E. Muxtariyyatin alda olunmasinda Naxcivanli diplomatlarin faaliyyati // AMEA NB "Xabarlar" jurnali, Naxgivan, 2016, No. 3, s. 127-138
33. Kalbizada E. Naxcivanin "tayini-muqaddarati" ugrunda Oli Sabri Qasimovun diplomatik faaliyyati // "Sarq qapisi" qazeti, 6 March 2014-cu il, No. 43 , s. 3
34. Kalbizada E. Siyasi proseslari milli maqsadlar istiqamatina yonaldan diplomat // "Sarq qapisi" qazeti, 16 March 2013-cu il, No. 50 , s. 3
35. Layos F. iran Sahlarinin iki Turkce Mektubu, TURKiYAT MECMUASI, Cilt V-VI (1934-36), s. 247-269
36. Qasimov O.S. Xatiralar, duygular. "Azarbaycan" jurnali, 1982, No. 1, s.162-163.
37. Quliyev M. Aman xan Naxcivanski: tanimali va tanitmali oldugumuz saxsiyyat, 525-ci qazet, 11 aprel 2013-cu il, s.7
38. Quliyev M. Behbud aga Sahtaxtinski haqqinda bazi qeydlar va yeni malumatlar // "Naxcivan" ictimai-siyasi, adabi-badii, elmi-publisistik jurnal, No. 23, Naxcivan, 2011, 207 s.
39. Quliyev M. Bir daha mashur harbici Aman xan Naxcivanski haqqinda // "Sarq qapisi" qazeti, 1 fevral 2013-cu il.
40. Quliyev M. Naxcivan xanliginin Qafqazda harbi-siyasi movqeyi va alaqalari. Naxcivan: Ocami, 2013, 184 s.
41. Quliyev M. Naxcivandan Varsavaya gedan Kangarli suvarilari haqqinda // Naxcivan Dovlat Universitetininin "Elmi asarlar "i; Naxcivan, 2010, № 1 (29), s. 9-11
42. Musayev i. Azarbaycanin Naxcivan va Zangazur bolgasinda siyasi vaziyyat va xarici dovlatlarin siyasati (1917-1921-ci illar), Baki: Baki Universiteti, 1996, s. 31-317. 314-317.
43. Naxcivan abidalari ensiklopediyasi. Naxcivan, 2008, 519 s.
44. Novruzov §. §arqi-Rusun gagiri§i. Baki:Yaziqi, 1988, 160 s.
45. Mahmudov Y.M. Azarbaycanin Avropa olkalari ila alaqalari. Agqoyunlu dovru (XV asrin II yarisi). Dars vasaiti. Baki: Tahsil, 2007, 116 s.
46. Pa§ayev A. Mahammad xan takinski kimdir? // Xalq qazeti. 18 iyul 2010, s. 6.
47. Pol§a Respublikasininin safirininin NMR-E safari, 29.09.-01.10.11 // Nyusleter

4/2011, Pol§a Respublikasininin Bakidaki Safirliyinin malumat bulliteni, 6 s.

48. Rahimov N. Balabay Qlibayovun Naxqivan Muzeyi // Naxqivan bu gun:islahatlar, perspektivlar (5-6 oktyabr 2007-ciilda kegirilmi§ beynalxalq simpoziumun materiallari), Baki: Nurlan, 2008, 548 s. s.185-188.

49. Sadiqov S. Naxqivan Muxtar Respublikasi tarixindan Baki, 1995, 144 s.

50. Safarli F. Behbud aga §ahtaxtinski gorkamli dovlat xadimi kimi // Naxqivan Dovlat Universitetininin "Elmi asarlar "i, ictimai elmlar seriyasi, 2012, No. 1 (45), s. 30-35

51. Safarli F. Behbud aga §ahtaxtinskinin hayati va faaliyyatininn bazi maqamlari haqqinda // "Naxqivan" ictimai-siyasi, adabi-badii, elmi publisistik jurnal. Naxqivan, 2011, No. 23, s. 7-18

52. Safarli F. Heydar Qliyev irsi - abadiya§ar talim. Naxqivan: Qcami, 2014, 200 s.

53. §ahtaxtli M. Taleyi va sanati:maqalalar / M. §ahtaxtli. Baki: Nurlan, 2008, 166 s.

54. §arif E. Kegmi§ gunlardan. Atam va man (Sanadli xatiralar), Baki: *Yaziqi*, 1983, 614 s.

55. Blamberg I. Vospominaniya, Moscow:Nauka, 1978, 356 p.

56. Gromyko A., Khvostov V. Documents of the Foreign Policy of the USSR 1924, Moscow: Politicheskaya Literatura, 1964, 759 p. (www.history-library.com)

57. Guliyev V. From the heritage of political emigration of Azerbaijan in Poland (30s of the twentieth century), Baku: Ozan, 2011, 548 pp

58. History before the revolution and memoirs, Moscow: Book, 1980, Vol. 3, Part 2, 367 p.

59. Kelbizadeh E. Bahram Khan of Nakhchivan: Foreign Minister of the Araz-Turkic Republic // Caspiy: Weekly Issue^ 19 Jun 2014, no.54, p.10 .

60. Kelbizadeh E. Life for the sake of the nation: three critical factors on the formation of Behbud Shahtakhtinsky as a diplomat // Caspiy: Weekly Issue^ 7 Jun 2014, no.50, p.10 .

61. Kelbizadeh E. Mohammed Khan of Teke: Foreign Minister of ADR // Caspiy: Weekly Issue^ 19 Jun 2014, no.54, p.10-11

62. Kelbizadeh E. Mohammed Khan of Teke: Foreign Minister of ADR // Caspiy:

Weekly, July 1, 2014, No. 59, p.10-11
63. Nagdaliyev F.F. Khans of Nakhchivan in the Russian Empire. Moscow: Novy Argument, 2006, 432 p.
64. RGVIA (Russian State Military Historical Archive), Fond 400, inventory 9, file No. 36040, doc. No. 10, Service List of Rahim Khan of Nakhichevan (23.08.1883)

CONTENTS.

Printed by Books on Demand GmbH, Norderstedt / Germany